W9-CEB-950

THE AIRPLANE

BY EMILY ROSE OACHS

Bellwether Media • Minneapolis, MN

Blastoff! Discovery launches
a new mission: reading to learn.
Filled with facts and features, each
book offers you an exciting new
world to explore!

This edition first published in 2019 by Bellwether Media, Inc.

No part of this publication may be reproduced in whole or in
part without written permission of the publisher.
For information regarding permission, write to Bellwether
Media, Inc., Attention: Permissions Department,
6012 Blue Circle Dr., Minnetonka, MN 55343.

Library of Congress Cataloging-in-Publication Data

Names: Oachs, Emily Rose, author.
Title: The Airplane / by Emily Rose Oachs.
Description: Minneapolis, MN : Bellwether Media, Inc., 2019.
   | Series: Blastoff! Discovery. Inventions that Changed the
   World | Includes bibliographical references and index. |
   Audience: Ages 7-13.
Identifiers: LCCN 2018040248 (print)
   | LCCN 2018041605 (ebook) | ISBN
   9781681036991 (ebook) | ISBN 9781626179653
   (hardcover : alk. paper) | ISBN 9781618915085
   (pbk. : alk. paper)
Subjects: LCSH: Aeronautics–History–Juvenile literature. |
   Airplanes–Juvenile literature.Classification: LCC TL547
   (ebook) | LCC TL547 .O23 2019 (print) | DDC
   629.133/34–dc23
LC record available at https://lccn.loc.gov/2018040248

Editor: Betsy Rathburn   Designer: Josh Brink

Printed in the United States of America, North Mankato, MN

TABLE OF CONTENTS

FALLING INTO FIRE

Orange flames lick the treetops, and smoke billows into the air. Miles away, a firefighter watches as an air tanker dumps red foam over the forest to slow the flames.

A siren sounds, and the firefighter pulls on her **parachute**, helmet, and other gear. She checks that everything is on tight. Then, she boards a small airplane with other firefighters. It is their turn to tackle the flames.

Soon, they are cruising above the fire. A spotter gives the firefighter a signal. She leaps from the plane. Others follow.

The firefighters fall toward the flames. Their parachutes open behind them, and they drop into a thick mountain forest at the fire's edge. More parachutes land beside them carrying the firefighting tools they will need. Without airplanes, nobody could have reached this area to fight the dangerous blaze!

DID YOU KNOW?

Skydiving firefighters are called smokejumpers. The U.S. Forest Service first started using smokejumpers to fight wildfires in 1940!

FIRST IN FLIGHT

People have studied human flight for centuries. Early flying machines had flapping wings like birds. In the 1400s, Leonardo da Vinci drew plans for one of these **ornithopters**. But they were unsuccessful.

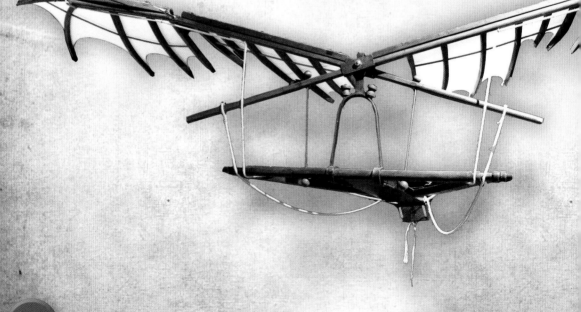

Leonardo da Vinci's ornithopter

Otto Lilienthal

By 1800, British inventor George Cayley suggested fixed wings for flying machines. His **aerodynamics** research led to new designs throughout the century. Otto Lilienthal created an aerodynamic wing design. Later, Samuel Langley created the aerodrome. It was the first self-powered flying machine!

WILBUR AND ORVILLE WRIGHT

Born: April 16, 1867, and August 19, 1871, in Dayton, Ohio

Background: Former bike and print shop owners who taught themselves about flying by studying other early airplanes

Airplane Invented: Wright Flyer I

Year Invented: 1903

Idea Development: The Wright brothers used discoveries from their early glider designs to build their first airplane with an engine. The Wright Flyer I became the first airplane to fly on December 17, 1903! More airplane designs followed.

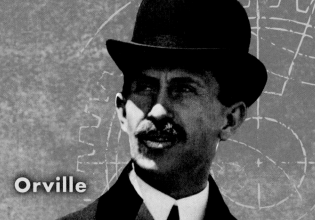

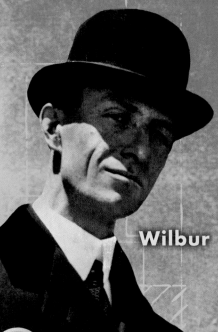

Wilbur

Orville

In 1899, Ohio brothers Wilbur and Orville Wright began their own flight experiments. The brothers closely examined the work of earlier **aviators** to create their own designs. On December 17, 1903, Orville piloted their Wright Flyer I 120 feet (37 meters) in 12 seconds. It was the first true airplane flight!

The Wright brothers' success gave people a bird's-eye view of the world around them. In time, long-distance travel became much faster. Journeys that once took two weeks by train or ship would take just hours by air!

Wright brothers' first flight

UNDERSTANDING AIRPLANES

Early aircraft were complicated machines. Inventors worked for many years to figure out how to build and fly them. To fly the Wright Flyer I, Orville laid across the plane's lower wing. Moving his hips controlled the **roll**, or the tilt, of the airplane's wings.

Orville's hips also shifted the **rudder**. This controlled the airplane's left and right movements. A lever changed the airplane's **pitch** by moving its nose up and down. The engine powered the **propellers**. These created **thrust** to drive the airplane forward.

AIRPLANES

Today's airplanes work just like those the Wright brothers flew. They even have the same parts! Propellers create thrust that moves the airplane forward. Steering instruments change the pitch, moving the airplane's nose up and down.

wing

rudder

thrust

pitch

thrust

propeller

ailerons

Over time, airplane designs continued to improve. The Wright Flyer III introduced a seat for both a pilot and a passenger. Its design became the basis for many later aircraft. In 1908, aviator Glenn Curtiss's June Bug plane featured an early use of **ailerons**. These movable flaps controlled the tilt of the plane's wings.

June Bug

Junkers J1

Early airplanes had wooden frames covered in fabric. The first all-metal aircraft was the 1915 Junkers J1. Metal made airplanes stronger and easier to maintain. The J1's new, thick wings also allowed the plane to carry more weight.

Advances in technology made flight easier and safer. During World War I, radios came on board. They allowed pilots to communicate with the ground and other airplanes. Soon after, early **navigation** systems were introduced.

DID YOU KNOW?

In 1927, pilot Charles Lindbergh boarded his airplane, *Spirit of St. Louis*, in New York. He crossed 3,610 miles (5,810 kilometers) to reach Paris, France. No one had ever before flown alone over the Atlantic Ocean!

Spirit of St. Louis

James Doolittle with his navigation system

These advances became increasingly important to aviators. In 1929, James Doolittle completed the first flight using only instruments for guidance. Pilots no longer needed to see to navigate. They could fly day or night! In the 1930s, aircraft began using **radar**. Radar helped pilots find nearby aircraft by using radio waves.

With the start of World War II, **engineers** worked to create more powerful engines. In 1939, Germany's Heinkel He 178 aircraft used the first jet engine. Inside the jet engine, gas and oxygen combined and started on fire. The burning gas blasted from the engine. Then, the airplane moved foward. Jet engines allowed airplanes to fly higher and faster!

DID YOU KNOW?

In May 1952, the de Havilland Comet took off from a London airport. In less than 24 hours, it carried its six crew members and 36 paying passengers to Johannesburg, South Africa. The Comet's journey marked the start of commercial jet travel!

Heinkel He 178

Boeing 307 Stratoliner

Higher flying meant new designs were needed. The 1940 Boeing 307 Stratoliner introduced the first **pressurized** cabin. This kept passengers safer while flying high in the air!

Thousands of different airplanes take to the skies each day. Each has a different purpose. Some, such as the Boeing 747, are airliners that carry hundreds of passengers. Freight planes are built to transport heavy loads of goods, such as mail, foods, and equipment. F-15 Eagles and other fighter jets fight enemy aircraft in the sky.

F-15 Eagle

Boeing 747

DID YOU KNOW?

In 2012, NASA needed to move the Space Shuttle Endeavour to its new home at the California Science Center. Engineers attached the space shuttle to the top of a Boeing 747. The Endeavour flew from Florida to Los Angeles this way!

Today, **GPS** technology helps with navigation. Pilots even have computers that automatically adjust the airplane's course and controls. Someday, computers may fully pilot airplanes!

TAKING TO THE SKIES

Airplanes bring the far reaches of the world together. They make it possible for people to eat food and wear clothes that come from distant countries. Packages and pieces of mail can circle the globe in days.

Airplanes also changed the way people get around. The first **commercial** airline opened in 1914. By 1957, more Americans were traveling on airplanes than on trains. Travel for business and fun became faster, easier, and more affordable. In 2017, nearly 4 billion passengers flew on commercial airlines worldwide!

AIRPLANE PROFILE

BOEING 747

Inventor's Name: Joe Sutter

Year of Release: 1969

Uses: The 747 is a huge commercial plane that can carry more than 500 passengers. It was the world's largest passenger airplane for nearly 40 years!

DID YOU KNOW?

The Boeing 747 is only made to carry about 500 people. But in 1991, a 747 carried 1,087 passengers at once!

The invention of airplanes also brought war to the skies. Pilots gather information or shoot down enemy aircraft. **Unmanned aerial vehicles** such as the General Atomics MQ-9 Reaper are becoming more commonplace. These can spy or fire on enemies without putting pilots at risk.

General Atomics MQ-9 Reaper

DID YOU KNOW

Hurricane hunters use special airplanes to find hurricanes. They steer into the hearts of hurricanes to collect information about the storms!

In the 1960s, scientists used airplane technology to build early spacecraft. If it were not for airplanes, Neil Armstrong may have never walked on the moon! Today, engineers are designing space planes. These vehicles take off and land like airplanes, but they fly beyond Earth's atmosphere!

THE FUTURE OF FLIGHT

Advanced technology promises to make commercial flight better for the planet. In 2013, the Solar Impulse crossed the United States powered only by solar energy. Experts believe that electric commercial airplanes are soon to come.

Solar Impulse

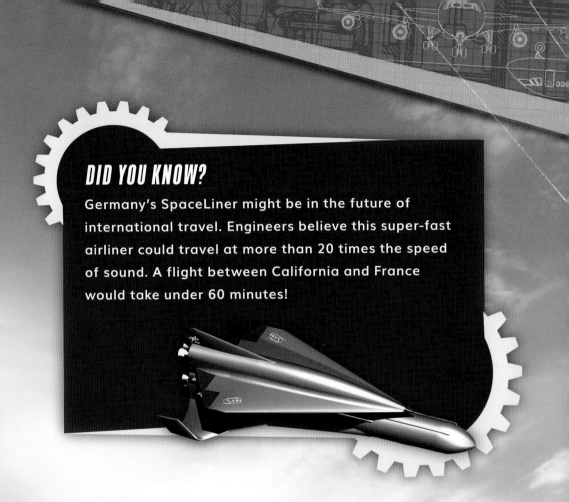

DID YOU KNOW?

Germany's SpaceLiner might be in the future of international travel. Engineers believe this super-fast airliner could travel at more than 20 times the speed of sound. A flight between California and France would take under 60 minutes!

The future may also hold flying cars, with some releases coming as early as 2019. UberAIR even plans to begin offering regular air taxi service in 2023! Today's engineers are working to push airplanes even further. With these advances on the horizon, airplanes might change the world all over again!

AIRPLANE TIMELINE

1505

Leonardo da Vinci designs a flying machine based on birds' wings

1903

The Wright brothers' Flyer I completes the first-ever powered, controlled, and piloted flight

1914

The first commercial flight travels between Tampa and St. Petersburg, Florida

1804

Sir George Cayley is the first to successfully build and test a glider

1908

The Wrights' Flyer III carries the first passenger

1929

The first flight using only instruments for guidance is made

1969

The spacecraft Apollo 11 reaches the moon

2019-

Future developments

2013

Airplane powered by solar energy flies across the United States

1939

Germany's Heinkel He 178 introduces the jet engine

GLOSSARY

aerodynamics—the study of how solid objects move through air

ailerons—movable flaps on an airplane's wings that control roll

aviators—people who fly airplanes, helicopters, and other aircraft

commercial—concerned with making a profit

engineers—people who design and build airplanes and other machines

GPS—global positioning system; GPS is a system that uses satellites to show an object's location.

navigation—the process of determining one's position and creating a route

ornithopters—machines designed to use flapping wings to copy how birds fly; ornithopters were not successful flying machines.

parachute—a device made of fabric that catches air to slow a fall

pitch—movement up and down

pressurized—maintaining normal amounts of pressure and oxygen in an airplane's cabin

propellers—fast-moving blades that are powered by an engine

radar—a system that uses radio waves to locate objects

roll—the tilting of an airplane's wings

rudder—a movable part at the back of an airplane that helps steer

thrust—forward force

unmanned aerial vehicles—airplanes that are piloted by computers or by people who are not on the airplane; unmanned aerial vehicles are sometimes called drones.

TO LEARN MORE

AT THE LIBRARY

Buckley, James, Jr. *Who Were the Wright Brothers?*
New York, N.Y.: Grosset & Dunlap, 2014.

Grove, Tim. *Milestones of Flight: From Hot Air
Balloons to SpaceShipOne*. New York, N.Y.: Abrams
Books for Young Readers, 2016.

Oxlade, Chris. *Inside Fighter Planes*. Minneapolis,
Minn.: Hungry Tomato, 2018.

ON THE WEB

Factsurfer.com gives you
a safe, fun way to find
more information.

1. Go to www.factsurfer.com.

2. Enter "airplane" into the search box.

3. Click the "Surf" button and select your
   book cover to see a list of related web sites.

INDEX